We Hardly See
 Each Other
Any More

Dad –

Another one of my
favorite books that
I hope you find time
to read. I hope you
enjoy it as much as I
do –
   Merry Christmas
        My Old Man –

l love you –

   Julie

We Hardly See Each Other Any More

Lee Philips

MERRIT MALLOY

A Dolphin Book
Doubleday & Company, Inc.
Garden City, New York

Jacket photograph Copyright © 1983 by Stephen R. Sanders

Library of Congress Cataloging in Publication Data

Malloy, Merrit.
  We hardly see each other any more.

  "A Dolphin book."
  I. Title.
PS3563.A4318W4   811'.54   AACR2
ISBN: 0-385-15944-7
Library of Congress Catalog Card Number 82–5082

In Celebration of
HENRY VALENTINE MILLER

"May God enjoy his company as much as we did. . . ."

Gail Mezey

I'd like to tip my hat to the following friends who came on the field with me in those last moments before publication and graciously offered the photographs that appear on these pages. If you were to ask me to name some of the honest pleasures in my life, surely each of these names would be among them . . .

Jeff Dunas
Geordie Hormel
Diana Levine
Charlie Malloy
Gail Mezey
Paul Monash
Linda Palmer
Caitlin Philips
Julie Philips
Lee Philips
Brian Roberts
Stephen Sanders
Len Steckler

And a special thanks to my old friends at Doubleday . . .

Lindy Hess
Debbie Parnon
Laura Van Wormer

Because books are made by hand

A NOTE FROM THE AUTHOR

This is not for you to feel
what *I* feel . . . But more
for you to feel what
you feel

I write from instinct
. . . I am not so skilled
that you might let me touch you
where you have not touched
yourself . . . So

It is not for me to take you
back to where *I*'ve been
But more . . . For you to take me
where *you*'re going

CONTENTS

We Hardly See
Each Other
Any More

THE ASKING

This book is an
asking

We are all the children
of children . . . And
all parents
were lovers
first . . . So

This page was written
with the prayer
that my children
might lift me out
of my Motherhood
one day

This is not to
tell them why . . .
But only
. . . How much

This book is an
asking

There is a very deep hand in me
that I never let you hold
when you were with me

. . . It is that same hand
that will not let you go of you
now that you're gone

Stephen R. Sanders

THE JOURNEY DOWN

Resentment
is just another way of
hanging on

As long as I hold you
in contempt
. . . I hold
you

So go on
. . . My freedom is dependent
upon yours
and

If I have to be alone
. . . I'd like to do it
by myself

A VIEW FROM THE FOXHOLE

. . . It is not an accident
that people get closer to us
as they leave . . . Especially
when we were afraid
they would

It is a corrupt blessing
But
. . . Everything comes
true

Caitlin Philips

SKIN POLKADOTS

Just as surely
as there is a time when
you get goosebumps
(those skin polkadots)
. . . There is a time when
you don't get goosebumps
any more

So don't lower your eyes
from the light
. . . Watch the scary parts
Go like the new kid
into the schoolyards
again . . . Because

Just as surely
as there is a time when
your heart misses a beat
. . . There is a time
when your heart
will miss them
all

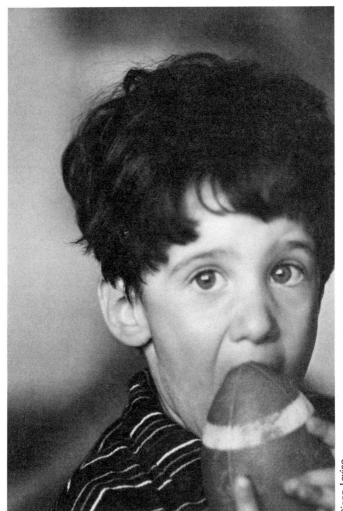

THE WEEK-END

The week-end
. . . It was awkward
clumsy
. . . It wasn't what I dreamed about
when I was ten.

It was better

Julie Philips

9

MIRACLE ON 58TH STREET

He built a trust
smile by smile
. . . Faith is a cellular
phenomenon

It was he who took off the bandages (those old clothes)
to let my body kiss nature
with its mouth open
. . . It gave me back
all my arms and
every one of them
were holding hands
with
him. (It was
a
sacrament)

My spirit was an
infant
again

This may not make the
papers . . . or break the safe reserve
around your heart . . . But
A great knife has been lifted
out of my childhood and

I am free
to dance in the
living room
again

Stone by stone
. . . He built a smile
Faith is a cellular
phenomenon . . . And

Trust is an
extra
arm

ALL NIGHT I COULD HEAR YOU COMING

All night
I could hear you coming
. . . Squeezing and stretching
kicking off the covers
like some adolescent boy
fighting the rapids
between your thighs
. . . I knew that sleep
could not keep you
for long

Your leg reaches around me
like a long arm
A young calf muscle
anchors just below my belly
. . . Your fingers look for me
with their eyes closed
The palm of your hand
cradles my ass
like a giant soup spoon
And here it comes (that sheet music)
the familiar rush of sweat and cologne
(that odd duet)

This morning your body
forces over the finish line in
some athletic hurry
. . . Your love had a
devil in it

. . . It makes you laugh
that I catch you
smiling

You pull me in to the curve of your groin
in one movement
as though I had handles on my sides
. . . Your chest kisses my back
and we connect below the ground somewhere
(skin roots)
The wet heat
steams us together
for that last hour's
rest

Your breathing is even now
the sun slices through a fold in the curtain
. . . Your muscles have no plans for awhile
Your hand fell asleep on my left breast
in that white meat just above my heart

. . . There is something perfectly rare
every time this happens and
I was thinking how odd it was
that my Mother used to be afraid
that a man would do
things like this
to me

I knew it the first time I saw him
. . . He had been there all along

A HARD THING TO SAY

"I love you"
That's a hard thing to say
for the first
time

It sticks in the
throat . . . A heart
birthing

The voice
(that old engine)
How easily it
can bruise
a wish

The mouth
is but
a
messenger

"I love you"
That's a hard thing to say
when you (finally)
mean
it

Paul Monash

17

A LONG TIME BURNING

You go on now
. . . I'll stay awhile
See that the fire is
out . . . It was
a long time burning

Hurry and you'll have
the house seats
on the ferry
at sunset . . . God takes
his red flag down
later in
the summer

It's all right
. . . I always wanted you
to go on ahead
of me . . . I always prayed
that you'd live the
longest

You can't fool me
. . . I know when the
seasons change
. . . I was born at
the end of September
. . . I know that
even men stop
bleeding

So you go ahead
. . . I promise I will sleep with you
again before I die
. . . Some night in an older room
you'll curl your legs up against
my side of the bed and
I'll take you down with me
on my last ride

For now . . . I'll
stay behind and
see that the fire is out
. . . It was a long time
burning

ONE OF THOSE MEN YOU COULD
NEVER UNDERSTAND

You are becoming one of the men
you always hated
The men who work for money
and brush their children's paintings aside
with a quick pat
on the head
. . . You are becoming one of the men
who want women who can't
surprise them
any more

You are turning old
. . . Last night you washed your hands
after making love
You are becoming one of those men
who get right out of bed
when the alarm clock rings
The men who bring flowers
only on
holidays

. . . You are becoming one of those men
you could never
understand

I WANT MY MONEY BACK

I want my money back
I want these five years returned
I want my memory repaired
. . . I want to be the girl
who loved you all her life
again

I want to stop knowing you
I want to leave you last summer
when you were still afraid
I would
. . . I want to be the girl
who couldn't

I want my money back

HIS LAST THREE SHIRTS

He took his last three
shirts this morning
. . . He didn't (actually)
say anything
He just reached into
the closet and took them
down from the shelf
. . . He checked the laundry
mark on the blue oxford cloth
to be sure it wasn't the one left over
from Paul . . . Both shirts
were exactly the same except
for the name
inside the
collar

He slipped the folded
three (no starch)
under his arm like
a notebook . . . With his other
hand he gently guided me
to his mouth and
gave me a businessman's
kiss

. . . Like I said
He didn't (actually)
say anything unusual
. . . Even his behavior wasn't
out of the ordinary . . . I
couldn't call it
memorable . . . Still
I know I won't ever (really)
be able to forget the morning
he took his last
three
shirts

THE FIRST TIME HE KISSED ME

The first time he kissed me
I pulled away
. . . I wasn't
ready

"I wish I were in love with you"
That's what I told him
. . . I wasn't yet and
I wanted to
be

The first night
we slept together
we didn't sleep
at all

The last time he kissed me
I pulled away
. . . I wasn't
ready

"I wish I were in love with you"
That's what I told him
. . . I wasn't any more
and I wanted to be

The last night
we slept together
we didn't wake up
at all

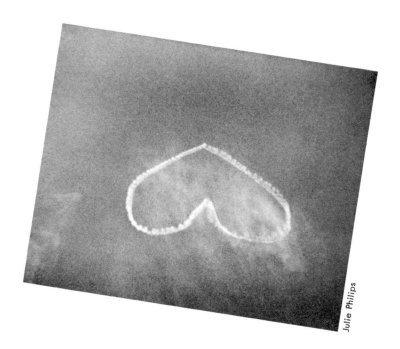

THE LOYALISTS

Loyalty is a slow dance
Not everyone can do it

It's not just a matter of faith
It's more than knowledge
Waiting for someone
is an instinct
. . . It can't be taught
or worn out or
even explained

Real loyalty
has absolutely no pride in it
and (I think)
it is made of
fur

Waiting (especially when nobody comes) is something
like love . . . Except it doesn't ever
end or stop
or change . . . And there is no language (not even cruelty)
that speaks against it

Dogs have died
waiting for people

Loyalty is a slow dance
. . . Not everyone can do it
It takes someone with that rare wisdom

that has no name and
doesn't ask to be
remembered . . . It is a wisdom
that has no competition in man
and because it has no rival

People have never died
waiting for dogs

PEOPLE LEAVE

People leave
. . . There is always
a chance of that
. . . It happens
But you mustn't be afraid
to say that
you don't
want them
to

It's true
. . . Sometimes people
don't come back
any more . . . But
that doesn't always
mean they don't
need you to ask
them to

There are lots
of people
who can't get home
but it doesn't hurt
to leave a key
under the
mat . . . Because

People come back
sometimes . . .

There is always
a chance of that
. . . It happens
And we mustn't be afraid
to tell them that
we always
hoped they
would

It's true
. . . There are a lot of people
who stay away forever
when all we had to do to bring
them home was ask them
to turn around

Lee Philips

THE PRICE

It wasn't that long ago
. . . We were young
and beautiful
and now we're only
young

Paul Monash

THE GIRL FROM BRIGHTON BEACH

Even though
I wasn't there
. . . He said I was the girl
he dreamed about
in Brighton Beach
(It didn't matter
that I'd never been
to Brooklyn)

Even though
he met me years too late
. . . He said I was his
childhood sweetheart
(It doesn't matter
that we were never young
together)

All lovers
are the same
age

And even though
I wasn't there
. . . I am the girl
he loved
in Brighton Beach

(It doesn't matter
that I was born twenty summers
later in another
town)

All lovers come
from the same
neighborhood

THE MAN WHO LOVED COLE PORTER

I can never be in New York again
without Lee
. . . Even when he's gone
I'll check for
messages

Each time I hear
a Cole Porter song
. . . A hand will squeeze me
just beneath the
tablecloth and
no matter where I am
or with whom
. . . I will be
with him
again

He is the man I loved
in the city
. . . Even when he's gone
I will save a seat for him
at the Carlyle Bar

Julie Philips

CATCH 22

One of the things
I lost
when you left
was the fear
of your
leaving

A WISH

I know that these words
aren't going to change your life . . . But
I thought they might
change your mind

THE TWENTY-THIRD POEM

I was lovely
because I lay in his
green pasture
. . . I was smart
because I told him
what he wanted
to hear . . . I was young
because his wife
was older

He called upon me
And . . . I
followed
. . . I was the lamb

The shepherd
was
My Lord

I ALWAYS BELIEVED IN YOU

I always believed in you
. . . Always counted you
would show 'em
. . . But that wasn't for
me to dream
. . . It's not my place
to make your
plans

Who am I
to seize your tiller
and lean against it
with all my
might? . . . Only time
can turn a battlefield
green

Whatever I did
for you . . . I did for
myself
. . . There was nothing
unconditional
about my generosity
and

I still believe
in you . . . Even though
it might tip your scales

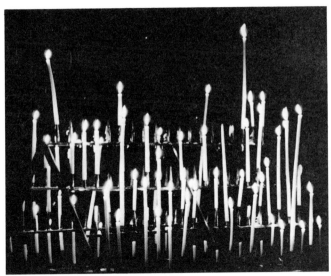

Stephen R. Sanders

I won't apologize
for my motives
. . . Your triumph is
a mutual
fund . . . And

Who is anyone
to say that faith
isn't a sound
investment?

A RESIDENT IN ABSENCE

The distance between us
is imperfect and
possessive . . . We are
nailed together by
a dream (yes, it was
amazing) . . . But

You knew I would come back
(I'm glad you didn't
ask me to) '

It might be better
(after all)
that I left still wanting
to stay . . . Than if
I stayed still wanting
to leave

The strangers circle
My mouth waits for them
like a bullseye . . . There is no
comfort in being
hunted . . . And my heart
is but a pilot
light

Julie Philips

WILL YOU LAY DOWN WITH ME

Will you
lay down with me
when my
womb is
in winter?
Will you pour
your sperm
into my last
campaign?
Will you want me
when freedom has
made a slave
of us . . . Or when
the neighbor boy
begs his small
white savior to
shame away my
years? . . . Will
you ask for my
wetness when
my moisture
doesn't come from nature or when
my words do not
enter you
with a poet's
ease?
Will you nail me
to the bed

like you do tonight
when all my charm
is turned to
character? . . . Oh,
will you wake up with me
when my womb is in
winter? . . . Will you press
against me in the morning
when it's been years
instead of hours since
I've stirred you in
the middle of
the night? . . . And will
you stay with me when
my face enters history?
Will you be there
when the bough breaks?
. . . Will you sleep with me
the night that I am
cured of your
desire?

THE NIGHT WE BURNED TO THE GROUND

I could have cried
but I didn't
There were obscenities I could have written on the walls
(I thought about that)
There were things I could have said
That would have broken somebody's heart
(Probably mine)

It's funny how the best of friends
sound insincere
on nights like these
No, I didn't call anybody
Being right
or charging sympathy
won't help
a girl
who's getting ready
to leave a man
who's already
gone

I DON'T MIND BEING ALONE

I don't mind
being alone
I just hate
the being left

The being over
isn't as bad as
the continuous
end

I don't mind
being alone
I am afraid that
your leaving me alone
will make me
hate you

What scares me
most is the
fear that
I'll always
be scared

This is where we turn
back into strangers again
This is what we were afraid of
all along
. . . This is
The hard
part

THE LAST CHURCH BEFORE WINTER

I'm pulling back a little
as I write this down
. . . My breath
is an
undertow

It doesn't help to know
that everybody comes to this
. . . It is not consoling
to know that there is competition
even in
breaking apart

. . . My devil
is deeper

All my knowledge
separates . . . My music
flies untethered
. . . My plans slam
against the walls
I am the blind
girl in a
fire

My work hurts
It's heavy . . . And my
style is entering science
There is a
brine of dishonesty
where I lay
my eggs

The cameras have
stared at me too long
My eyes suck at the
lens and my smile
is play money

. . . My devil
is
deeper

I want to feel
something for the first time
again . . . I want
to be comforted with
apples

Is this the last church before winter?
My wine does not turn into the
blood of Christ . . . And my devotion
is a bucket of
holes

WHEN

When did we start
to care more about
what people thought
about us
than
what we felt
for
each other?

BIOGRAPHY

The truth isn't
what happens
Not what 'really'
happens . . . Nah
The truth is
what we
remember . . . Because
what we
remember
happens
again

The truth
isn't 'fact'
Facts are names and
dates and
things that
'actually'
happened then
. . . The truth
is how
we feel
about it
now

FREEDOM

I'm free
when I'm with
someone I love
. . . Attachments
release
me

Giving someone
my love
frees me from
the search
to find someone
I can give
my love
to

Freedom isn't
being alone
all the time . . . Freedom
is being alone
when we want
to be
alone . . . So

Go on and
ride the trails
. . . Your fury is not
so amazing

. . . Isn't
independence just
another tyrant? . . . All
you are 'free' to do
is search for someone
to come home to
again

Isn't asking
for freedom (often)
just a beg for the
opportunity to be
captured
again?

LOVE JUST ISN'T ENOUGH ANY MORE

I can't twist logic
or heal you
(completely)
from the
network
news

. . . I'm afraid to say
that love just
isn't enough
any more . . . It takes
faith to
repair
thought

There is
nothing remarkable
about
passing judgment
Opinion has never
cured a single
street of
imperfection . . . And

Comes a day
when you know you
knew you knew it
all
along

. . . Love just
isn't enough
any more . . . It
takes faith
to
twist
logic and
repair human
thought

PASSING THROUGH

There are no strangers
. . . There are just people
who we don't know yet
or don't know
any more

Julie Philips

59

THE DIFFERENCE BETWEEN MEN AND WOMEN

Men want to go to bed
with women and
women want to wake up
with men

You see
lovers are born too
Just like regular people
Except that
women are girls
first and
men become
boys

It happens early on
. . . Little girls will always
touch you
if you love them and
little boys will always love you
if you touch them

It's the same
difference

PLEASE COME DOWN

Please
come down
Don't make me
bleed
you . . . Yes
you can touch
me where I
smile . . . It is
your
wound

Come down
please
. . . I'll give you
the gun
I won't hurt
you where
you
cry . . . Please

come down
. . . Enter my wetness
like a
boy
I will stay
up north
like a
virgin

Please . . . My mouth
is a baby tonight
. . . It
searches in the
dark for
any Mother . . . Let my
hair fall
on your
belly . . . I won't
bite you
where you
die . . . Please

unclothe me to
my first communion
. . . Take me further
Take me
deeper . . . But
never take me
back . . . Please
don't make
me bleed
you . . . I can touch
you where
you
smile . . . It is
my wound

LEAVING

For a while now
(maybe more than that)
I've been thinking
of leaving

Every day I check
the balance . . . I wonder
how the world
might accept me
if I got out?

He might have
paroled me
if I asked
(But it isn't
something you
ask for)
Each crime
obeys the
law (paid for
or not) . . . Justice
isn't perfect
It is still a business
run by
people

I've been thinking
of leaving
There is no grace
to it
. . . It has the
deceit of hospital
corridors where
relatives whisper
funeral arrangements
(It is wrong to
speed breathing)
There is a morality
that governs each
crossroad

Each crime has its
law . . . You can damn me
for giving you
hope . . . But
we are all waiting in line . . . And
For a while now
(maybe more than that)
you've been thinking
of leaving

Stephen R. Sanders

WE WANTED IT ALL

We wanted it all, didn't we?
We demanded magic
(as if spontaneity could be planned)
We demanded perfect freedom and safety both
(how had we ever dreamed
of corrupting natural law?)

We were the great believers
(It was our strength and
our weakness)
Who would have guessed
that the very love that
brought us together would
break our hearts?

And here we are again
This time in a rage
for peace
(as though virtue could
be assembled)

Even in the end
. . . We want it all
We demand a leaving made
of affection (as though poverty
was ever cured by
good intentions)

There is no redemption
in a decent memorial
(Charlie is still
dead)

YES, WE ARE LOSING EACH OTHER

Yes, we are losing
each other . . . It is
grief enough
to force anyone
to bitterness . . . But
there is a sovereignty
in people who have
fought the world
together . . . It is
that root of loyalty
I dig for now . . . The
heart is a
prospector

Sure we've had
better times . . . But
none more memorable
as these . . . How can
we easily forget
how much it hurts
when the devil
enters the mouth
we loved and
spits out desire
like a dead egg
Is there no
amnesty for
lovers? . . . *Must we*

still be afraid
of death even
in hell?

Yes, we are losing
each other . . . It is
grief enough to
make us mean . . . Still
there is a sovereignty
in people who have
held each other
through the night . . . It
is that old friendship
that I treasure most
. . . I am a
patriot

I want you to
know that
even now when you
least dreamed it
I am your
comrade and
Every time you
raise your weapon
I will be
at your
side

Just this
once could we
be tender with
each other? . . . Could we
be extravagant
this time . . . not let
the spirit harden
and make
fists . . . there is
a miracle in breaking
down . . . there is
an utter dignity
in the cracking
of a
voice . . . Did you
know that I loved
you most that night
when you cried and
told me about
your
Father?

Diana Levine

HOW COME IT STILL HURTS?

You say we have
nothing to lose
with each other . . . Then
how come it still
hurts?

You walk out the
door or hang up
the phone and
a knife slams
into my
gut . . . Slap!
My heart begs you
not to hit
it
again . . . Please

You say we have
nothing to
lose . . . Then how
come it
still
hurts?

How come you
come back when
there is
nothing left
to leave? . . .
turn away and
you squeeze my
arm leaving broken
veins on my
handshake . . . Please

You say we have
nothing to lose
any more . . . Then
how come we're
still
losing?

THE THINGS PEOPLE DO TO EACH OTHER WHEN THEY'RE SCARED

Aggression
Contempt
Cynicism
Aren't they
just the children
of isolation?
Aren't we just
two lonely
people?
Isn't *fear*
our biggest
fear and isn't
pain the
original
anger?

HOW LOVE WORKS

You say that love doesn't work
But it does work
It works hard

Love isn't something you can fall into . . . It's a way of life
. . . Life is a journey
Not a destination
So . . . How can

you say that love doesn't work?
. . . It does work
It works
hard

It just didn't
work for
us

How long has it been
since I've written you those midnight notes?
(Those passion plays)
How long since you've stuffed
them in your jeans pocket
to read
like a thief
at home? . . . How long
since a call from me
has stirred the
groin?

You have stuck in my mind
for four years
like a blood clot
Like some romantic
time bomb
My loyalty
explodes . . . Is this
supposed to be the night
I can't go
on?

Remember when anything
was possible? . . . Our nerves
were awake . . . There was
no pain that could

penetrate
the glands . . . But
Guilt was the sniper
Waiting like a savage
(It turned your heart
to ash)

How long has it been
since you've lived like a squatter
on my body's land? . . . How long
since your hind legs
reared?

"Touch me" you said
"But not too much" . . . And "Take me"
"But not too far" . . . Pride was
   the tyrant . . . Waiting
   like a parent . . . (How long since
   anything has brought you
   to your
   knees?)

IRONIC, ISN'T IT?

Ironic, isn't it?
That this should happen so close to
Memorial Day

It's no wonder to me now
That you're afraid you'll die alone
in an unloved room

There is a lot I can't say
. . . There is no virtue in being versed in the confessional

I will soon forget the look in your eyes when you loved me
. . . When the honor system worked

What was I anyway?
An armful of air
. . . A passing fancy . . . And in time
I go . . . ?

God help you
Because some voice in you
has always been
asking for
more

This is the actual pulling of the trigger
Bang/Bang we're dead!
An emotional economy

We are a disgrace
as lovers
A tragic passion
without dancers

We took miracles
and made them common
We dishonored faith
And . . . We have corrupted the sacrament
of holding hands

Did you really think I was going to pretend
you were worth it?
. . . Did you really expect me to be
polite????

LETTING IT HIT THE FAN

Did you think
I would bite my lip and
let you go
without a
fight?

Did you really think
I could let my spirit
go limp?
Or . . . Let my love
get flabby?

Did you hope that I
would say that you were
classical? . . . Nah
I'm going to let it
hit the fan

After all
it's just a piece of business
I can escape your
absence
. . . It's a criminal thought
But we are all murderers
under the right
circumstances

It is corny and cruel
and below the belt
But it will be a
solemn pleasure
to live without
you and

I will pretend it
doesn't matter until
it really
doesn't

I AM SADLY PROUD

I am sadly
proud that
the ladies see
how beautiful he is
I never thought
I would say
this . . . But
I'll pray that their
love will heal
him from
mine . . . But
I'll never be
happy about
it

I SAW YOU TONIGHT

I saw you tonight
. . . You were with a girl
I could have called to you
But what to say?
. . . That my eyes were
these reluctant thieves?
. . . That some innocent design
had brought our cars to rest
side by side at a
three-way light?

I looked across
(a Peeping Tom)
from the passing lane
You were spilling out
a good belly laugh
(those sweet familiar ribbons)
My spirit caught your
fire again and

It wasn't until later that
I remembered how I rubbed
cream into those flesh leather
seats of yours . . . My earrings
were in the glove compartment
where the registration still
bears my name . . . Oh,
it was perfect

You jumped the light
rushing
on your way up the hill
to my old bed
with her . . . Leaving me
an unwilling voyeur
My heart
was a
beggar

THAT SQUEEZE

That squeeze was
a warning
Our love was
bleeding even
then, wasn't
it?

There was a kindness
in both of us that day
(a severance pay)
the poignancy
of a smile
rooted in
regret

          "C'mon" I said . . . "Why don't we
          go to bed and
          visit home?"

FRESH STRAWBERRIES

There were fresh strawberries
in the market
this morning
. . . I guess we didn't make it
through the winter
this year

THE CHECK

I always figured
this time would come.
Somebody would
place a check on
the tables where we
held hands and
drank white
wine

We might have
slipped through
the barbed wire . . . Over
that kharmic border
to safety . . . Fat
chance, huh . . . that
a waiter's memory might
endear him to
us at closing time?

I always
figured we'd have to
pay eventually . . . But
not so
soon and
not so
much

It's astounding
to me
how expensive things are
these days and
how little wine it takes
to reduce the
price of
anything
(It's not only
amazing how quickly one
forgets but
how much!)

SOMETIMES WE HAVE TO GO BACK

Sometimes we have to go back
And wake up with somebody again
Before we know
That we don't want to
Wake up with them
Any more

It was a primitive gesture
A late payment for some
breaking down . . . I opened my memory
and squeezed the last of our dream
on him . . . He poured back
into me . . . And
changed the past
forever

It was a human sin
(not even a big one as sins go)
At the time
I saw some justice in it
. . . There is some kharmic
perfection
in trembling against your husband
Afraid . . . That your lover
might find
out

EVERYTHING I HAD

Hard to believe it now . . . But
there was a time
when I would have given you
everything I had
. . . Trouble is
I did

THE MEANEST THING

The meanest thing
isn't leaving
. . . It's coming back
And leaving
again

I SHOULDA TOLD HIM

I shoulda told him
right away . . . But
I couldn't

You shoulda seen his face
He was like a boy soldier
Anxious to claim his
native soil . . . So grateful
to be home alive
again

"I want us to be old together, huh?"
"We'll have an attic and
a porch" . . . that's what he said
(He meant it)

He knew I would wait for him
and I did
So
How could I tell him
that it wasn't
long enough?

You shoulda seen his face
It was just like mine
usta be

YOUR STORY

I have no wish to
censor you
This story is
yours . . . But

It is lonely to be
misunderstood . . . to be
paralyzed into your
future without
the talent of
distinguishing
your past

I refuse historical
compromise
It was that instinct in me
that you loved
and hated

This is not
bar room
conversation
. . . You can't determine
what I am (to you) now
without consulting what
I was (to you)
then

Even you cannot
convict me of evil
thoughts I didn't
even think
of

You can take my
good-bys and
string them around
your tree but
you can't set your years with me
on fire

This is your
story and I have no wish
to censor you
. . . History will
repeat enough
of
that

HOW I LEARNED HOW TO LIVE ALONE

I won't cry
Crying never brought
anybody back
(for long)

I'll be all right
. . . I've learned
how to live alone
by living
with
you

1983

It's 1983
. . . Time has grown
rings around us and
George Orwell
will (finally)
have his day

'Good-by' is an
unnecessary word . . . It
is not something you
can say . . . It is only something
you can do

Really blessed friends
come just as rarely as
true lovers . . . and
since there is some
reluctance in the
seed . . . Could we
remove our hands
from the neck of the
flowers?

It is 1983
and
"Good-by" is
an unnecessary
word

JUST LIKE EVERYONE ELSE

I used to dream
about
driving a car
. . . I was never
going to
be sixteen
(Those last six
months were the
longest in my
life until
now)

I never thought
I'd be able to
have a quiet
drink without
offering
proof that
I was
born . . . (and
when)

And marriage?
. . . Who would marry
me? . . . A girl
who sleeps too
late and dreams
too much? (innocence
was my only charm)

I used to pray
to be just like everyone else
. . . I should have
been more
careful

Funny how
most of what we don't want
any more
is what we used to want
most of all?

I HURT HIM BAD THIS TIME

I hurt him bad
this time

I wish he could beat me up
or something
. . . A good spanking usta hurt like hell
But it always brought
redemption, didn't it?
Each slap brought me closer
to innocence
. . . Each cry was testimony to
payment . . . But

These are not childhood sins
And this time
. . . I really hurt him
bad

If only I could tell a priest
Take my punishment
Like the Catholics
. . . I would gladly kneel here
and follow the dotted lines
of my rosary again . . . But
he won't forgive me
As easily as God . . . And

I hurt him bad
this time

Linda Palmer

DAVID

David
has the most beautiful eyes
Not so much for what
you'll see when you look
at *them* . . . But
for what *they* will
see when they look
at you

PAUL

I don't hear much from Paul
any more . . . He learned silence
and anarchy from
being an only
child
(Weren't we
all?)

Is he still within
the reach of God? . . . And
will he love another Merrit
in the end?

It's not like he didn't
warn me . . . there would be these
flashes of feeling
(intermittent thunder)
a scribble of regret

Does he still have his
boyskin . . . that sweet
unlaundered laugh? . . . or does
he take smaller steps?
Careful now not to take
too many?

We say a lot
But loneliness will change
our minds . . . It
always does

Cream rises
. . . It is nature's law
I have no wish to
distract science . . . But *I* am
still within the reach of
God and . . . My green robe hangs
in Paul's closet
like an Irish
scar

ANNE

Anne . . . Please
don't let them take you
now . . . I promise
I will never say good-by
for you
. . . I won't
I'll keep your phone number
in my book and
save your skate key . . . Anne
I won't let you go
Not like this
Not now

It can't be true
that I can't talk to you
any more . . . That your face
is dead . . . Annie
It can't be true
that all your eyes
are closed . . . That
all our plans are
useless

Oh no, I won't let you
break my heart
like this . . . You've been
my closest pal for

all these years . . . I
loved you, Anne . . . Please
don't let them take you
now

. . . Alexander's only four
Far too soon to push him
from your Mother fur
. . . Anne
Whole landscapes of the past
are lost . . . And
I will not let you go
I'll get down on my hands
and knees . . . I'll pay them
anything they want . . . I'll
make a deal . . . But
I won't let them
take you . . . Not this early
and . . . not like
this . . . Anne please
. . . If I'm never to see you again
What am I to do
with all this
love?

OH, WE COULD TELL THEM STORIES

Oh, we could tell them
stories, couldn't we?
. . . We could bring down
the house
. . . Song by song
Mouth to mouth
and down
the mountainside

We prayed the prayers
right off the Jesuits
you and me
The nuns waited
like bounty
hunters (Their vows
hurt them and
demanded
everything)

. . . There is no
prayer that can
comfort a
Catholic girl
who hears the
wrath of God
beneath the hands
of
men . . . Oh

We could tell you stories
. . . We could take our past
and distribute it
among the bored . . .
It won't count in the world
or matter to the historians . . . But
once . . . We declared an independence
We separated church and
state . . . We fell
on our knees and still
had the feminists
behind us . . . Oh

They told us that
death was inescapable
but life wasn't . . . Life was
something that you had to
ask for and earn
. . . Song by song
Mouth to mouth
and down the
mountainside

There is no prayer
that will redeem a
Catholic girl who has no sin
to be sorry for

ALEXANDER

Dear Alexander
. . . You don't know me
We did meet briefly
when you were born
(But that was four years ago
and you may not
remember)

I have to write this down
even though it will be years
before you come to know me
and longer still
before these words
have found
a
home

I really loved her
(Your Mother) For most
of my life she was my pal
. . . May you have some
comfort in knowing
that you are the son of
a woman who
loved men . . . You are the
child of a Mother
who rejoiced in
children . . . It may be

a grand inheritance (after all)
to have come here
through the body of a woman
who had a sincere respect
for life

There comes a natural leaving for
most children . . . a begging to be released
Your time came sooner than later
(stolen from your natural brine)
and you didn't even ask . . . I
cannot take away your vacancy
or rock away your childhood grief . . . But
I can tell you that
your Mother only wanted to bring you here so
that she might set you free
not keep you . . . So go on and be free, Alexander
That is the only dream she ever dreamed
that always stayed the same

. . . You won't recognize me when I see you again
I'm sure of that . . . But I've been four years old myself
And I want you to know that I'm sorry that I knew
your Mother longer than you did . . . If I could
I'd like to give you all of her I have
so that you might celebrate her life with me
. . . So that we might set *her* free
To enter *your* life again with joy

as *you* entered *hers* . . . Until that day
I will pray for you with every voice I have

Dear Alexander
Won't you let me be
your heart's magician?
We will learn together
how to live
in a world
without an
Anne

Diana Levine

BILL

I shall never be able
to reach back and hold you
with last year's arms . . . But
I am that girl you imagined
getting off that boat in
Barcelona . . . I am the
pink fish virgin . . . Born
from my Mother's
water . . . And

I am not afraid to be
anywhere I am
. . . I am just reluctant
to be imagined

There is something final
in the way you push the paint
across the page . . . You
have genuine hands, Bill
No one will forgive you
the original dream and
no whiskey is gonna
get to it
Before you
do

. . . Like you
I toil in the fields
Making a harvest
out of air . . . Fighting
like hell not to
be imagined . . . and always
(yeah)
. . . Always on a
boat to
Spain

JAMES

His name was James
And he wrote me a poem
that I never read
. . . But
I'll always remember
it

. . . "I was his
Carole Lombard" . . . that's
how his Mother
put it . . . She's
almost sixty now and
she talks to
me of Churchill
as if I'd
been
there

His name was
James . . . they never
called him
Jimmy . . . He was born
for them from
the war (the second big one)
. . . He was tall but
he never got
very
old

. . . He loved Bogart
and Gable . . . They were
his muscles . . . He was
just as glib as
Brando and just as
inaccessible

. . . He lived in a chair
He was governed by
the wheels . . . But in
the afternoons at two exactly
. . . He borrowed the gifted flight of
Fred Astaire and forced
his forgotten legs
to say a grace
that never
reached the
ground

"I was his Carole
   Lombard" . . . that's how his
   Mother put it . . . And she talks to me
   of early death and tragedy as though
   I could forget a boy named
   James who lived in
   a chair

MCCHESNEY

McChesney is her
name . . . (one of them)
I just call her
Marilyn . . . (I'm funny
that way)

She says
"there are no intelligent
women when it
comes to
men" . . . (she's right
about that
last
part)

I didn't count
on this
blessing, you
know? . . . To
have myself
a genuine
crony . . . wouldn't
you know she's a
Yankee too . . . As
Irish as
Boston and
just as
lucky

She doesn't give
up or give in
. . . She is
innocent and
terrible
(like me)
We're cronies
There is
a distinction
in this (we are set
apart from
hooligans . . . let's
say) . . . A "crony" (doncha know) talks like a
Sullivan cop (I hope ya's had one
like my Uncle Paddy) . . . And a crony
is an accomplice (yeah)
A Marilyn

She just
passed all
my defenses
and entered
my memory without
a
splash . . . It
was very
subtle . . . and

of course, it was
magic . . . So
(I promised not
to tell you
about the
good
stuff)

Marilyn knows
too much (especially about me)
(especially about
you know
what) . . . But she doesn't
have a flair for
blackmail and
Revenge has
never been one
of her
charms

She believes in
Heaven . . . (She thinks
it's just good
sense) . . . She's too smart
to question
anyone who walks

on
water . . . I'm telling
you, she's smart . . . And
another thing
She's sincere
She will defend you
(even if you're
wrong) . . . Her loyalty
is not just
another military
band

Who would
ever
believe it? . . . That
once again my life
and times could bear
another growing up
and give me
back another
Anne . . . (Oh no,
there is no similarity
except when the
chips are
down) . . . Some of the
stories would
break your

heart if they
weren't so
funny . . . (especially
the one about
what's her
name). . . I'm
telling you

. . . Her name is
McChesney (has a nice ring,
don't you think?) but
I call her
Marilyn . . . (She'll get used to it) . . . She's
one of my
cronies doncha
know?
One of the
guys only
some of us are
girls

We will meet
you at The White
Horse . . . we'll match you
lie for lie right under
the table . . . We are the girls
who made you cry and we
are out to ride the

last frontier . . . Hoping
that Dylan or
O'Casey might be out
there . . . I always thought
they'd hide a pint or
two (for the night they charm Jesus into
letting 'em back) . . . Those are two
fellas who would know a
genuine crony if they
saw one . . . (doncha know?)

COOPER, PH.D.

Her name is Cooper
She is a human guide
Instinctive and
Blind

You can't side-step her
. . . You have no charm
that can distract her
from your
Corruption

She will wait for you
Even if you don't come
Even if you don't
Care . . . And

You can't side-step her
. . . You have no pain
that can distract her
from your
beauty

BANDITS AND OLD AGE

I hope you'll
answer me, Lee
. . . I hope you will
open to this page someday and
try to find me
if you can

I hope you'll forgive me
for writing it
down . . . But what other
hand did I have to
reach out ahead
of our time?
. . . I wanted you to know
each time you pulled
this from your shelf
I might be alive somewhere
. . . And if I am
I'd like to talk with you
of old age and bandits
. . . I could be living in
the Vineyard (it has always
been my dream) . . . Remember how
I begged you to take me
back to Edgartown?
I hope you'll forgive me

for going back alone . . . Each choice
has its own heart . . . I wish
that you would come to me
even when it is too late
to come back . . . What's another chance
to you and me
. . . We have had so
many

Paul
. . . You have used me to
protect yourself
from other women
. . . You have used other women
to protect yourself
from me
. . . Safety is
no anchorage for a
man like you
. . . Standing still
is no definition
for madness
. . . The middle ground
has no name for
passion . . . And
Movement is not something
you can keep
at arm's length

I have similar battles
(life and death
among them) . . . But
that is a natural competition
. . . I crowned you
for teaching me to
trust excitement

. . . You blessed me
with a fighting
chance

My children ran with us
An awkward third leg
limping to the altar
. . . Do you recall how hard we tried
and how we couldn't make our
devotion comparative?

Safety is no anchorage
for you, Paul . . . There is no
delight in being a

hostage at home . . . I never
meant to curse you . . . But
saving time never works
and all your money
will be useless when
the pain comes . . . So

Trust your own excitement, Paul
. . . And if you must protect yourself
protect yourself from safety . . . Because
it is no anchorage for
a man like
you

I KNOW I CAN HURT YOU

I know I can
hurt you . . . But
I won't
Not just to be
romantic or
give you
pain enough to
write your
novels

I like you . . .
I know that doesn't fit your plans
And
If you want me to
be jealous . . . You
can't do it with
other girls . . . You can only
do that by writing (or doing)
something magnificent
. . . I can only envy
something I dreamed
for
myself . . . But

Jealous of an
old girlfriend?

Not me! I've been
an old girlfriend
(that atrophied
miracle) . . . Hey

She isn't me
and . . . I'm
not her . . . That's why
I'm here and
she
isn't . . . So
no . . . I won't leave
you . . . not just to
be romantic or
give you
pain enough to
write . . . You can't
do anything to
me that I haven't
done to
somebody
else

I know I can hurt you
But I
won't

TONY

Tony said he
didn't believe in
poetry . . . He said that
romance was a children's
crime . . . He saw
sorrow and
celebration both
as creative
enterprise

Being in love
was simply creating
a whining need
and another
problem . . . He did it
once . . . It was a whim
She was a dancer
wed to the
six
positions . . . She wore
a red railroad scarf and
drove (too fast) a white
VW convertible

He says he listens
to music . . . But not
the words . . . That he goes
to films but knows

that they're only
movies . . . But today a
white VW caught his eye
as we pulled
off of Sunset . . . He
stretched to check the
driver for a red scarf
(it wasn't her)
. . . He says he
doesn't care any more
but

Tony doesn't always say what he
means . . . If you listen
he'll always tell you
the truth . . . He has an old
dog name of 'Hidden' who
he picked up from the pound (scared) and who he
taught to laugh . . . He'll always
remember your birthday and
pick up your messages . . . even though to be
a friend (he says) is a
cruel and unrealistic
demand (he's one of the best)
. . . Tony gives me a lot
of the poetry
he doesn't
believe in

Stephen R. Sanders

135

FOR ALL THE FRIENDS I HAVE THAT I DON'T KNOW

Who are you
that I've come to touch you
like this . . . You
who write me letters
that can only come from
friends?

You say you've met me
in the dark? . . . That
in reaching for myself
I formed a family
and held again
those whom I never held
before?

What a perfect irony it is
That you should grant me
entrance into your arms . . . When
the arms of the people
for whom these pages were written
are closed to me
forever?

And who am I
to say that all friends
must be strangers
first?

Brian Roberts

137

LINDSEY

Lindsey lives alone
She says that's how she likes it
(she's lying)

She has never sent a man roses
She says women aren't supposed to
She says it intimidates them
(she's wrong)

Lindsey needs a place to work alone
A place where she can have a secret drawer
She says men don't understand that
(she never asked them to)

Lindsey likes to touch women now
She says it feels better
(safer anyway)
She says she doesn't miss the smell of a man
She says it doesn't matter at all
that it doesn't hurt any more
(but it does)

Lindsey keeps his key ring
like a relic in her night table
(second drawer) . . . He said he'd come back for it
(he didn't). So

Lindsey lives alone
She says she won't compromise for anyone
Or give up her freedom
(she already has)

STEVEN

He wrote a
song . . . My friend
Steven

He wrote it
for Dominique . . . To
bring her
home . . . It was
an open
hand

He sold a
million copies . . . the
radio said
his prayers . . . and
he was heard
in every home
but his
own

It was a sad
success for
Steven . . . The song
brought him glory and
made him rich
(except) in
everything
he didn't
have

He wrote
the song for
Dominique . . . To
bring her
home . . . It was
an open
hand . . . It touched
everyone but
her . . . So

Steven is
an accidental
Jesus to the
teenage heart . . . He is a
sincere liar
He asks the
crowd to be a
woman . . . And now he
sleeps awake with
everyone except
his own

THE SUMMER OF OUR DISCONTENT

I heard him crying today
all wet like that/I couldn't let him go
I felt him enter my
family/right there in
the kitchen/all legs
and heart/For all his years
He was my third-grade love
back again to write me unscrubbed
letters/His love was sore and
young and very red/

"Please stay with me?"
All wet like that/I couldn't let
him go/He was my harp seal
All moist and trusting
These are
slippery times

I cannot let him go/He is
all that's left of
my wing and I am cured
of everything but
flying

MAMA, I WAS THIRTY TODAY

Mama
I was thirty today
. . . you should see
what's become of
your pink
child . . . I would
hardly leave you
with the dishes
now

I always thought
that we'd be pals
That you might
live to see
my dreams
breathe . . . That
I might live
to see you love
another
Charlie

Mama . . . I was
thirty today
Anne is gone and
so is Bridgie . . . We
are left to
trim the trees
alone

(I always miss you
most of all on
Christmas
Eve)

I always prayed
that you'd be here
when all my notebooks
came true . . . When
all the things they
said I couldn't do
were
done (Remember how
you kept my poems
in your jewelry
box? . . . folded in that
satin drawer?)
I'm so sorry for
the times you came
upstairs and
I wouldn't let
you
in

Mama
. . . I was thirty
today . . . Tally lives
in Spain and Peter

Charlie Malloy

has a son
named Michael
(wouldn't you know)
Suzanne is a
woman now . . . She
goes to school in
Paris . . . (Remember
when you wouldn't
let her
cross the
street?)

I always thought
that you'd be here
when we got home
that you might live
to see the songs
your faith wrote
in all of us
. . . I always prayed
that you might live
to see me
as a woman and that
I might live to
hold you
like a
friend

Hardly anybody
stays forever
any more . . . But
I always thought that
we'd be different
I never dreamed that
I would (finally)
have the passage home and
be left like this
without a
destination

I was thirty today
Mama . . . It's been a long
time since you've rubbed
Vicks on my chest . . . But
I would hardly
put up a fight
about it
now

SOMETHING I WROTE DOWN ON THE NIGHT SHE LEFT

Helen
They wrote your
name on a card
They attached
it to your right
ankle . . . (they
tied a 'double' knot
in the string) . . . it pinched an accordion in your skin . . .
I saw them do it (I didn't want to)
They took you (without a
fight) into their basement
where you entered inventory and waited
for delivery
home (your
last one)

I never could
understand how
you could get
intensive care
from strangers

Helen
They let me see
you the day you
left us . . . You were
busy packing

Charlie Malloy

(you didn't fool
me) . . . You knew I
was there . . . You heard me
yelling . . . I wasn't
very considerate
was I? . . . Trying

to interfere with
your plans again . . . I
never liked it
when you went
away

. . . I was always
afraid that
you wouldn't
come
back!

THE MAN WHO FIRST TOUCHED ME

The man
who first touched me
doesn't press against the body
of a woman
any more

. . . His eyes
(those blue cameras)
They don't break
the same commandments
now

He moves among us
like a blind bumper car
. . . His friends
(even the season ticket
holders) . . . They enter
him like a man . . . And
leave

I think of how
he might read this
and lean away from the
page . . . His eyebrows
speak soliloquies

Tonight
I sat sidesaddle on his chest

beating my wings against
the air as he
let his hair fall to shadow
his eyes and hid
beneath those
covers

These thoughts come
from the wild . . . His heart
beats a cricket sound
under the shell of his
chest . . . He held on
to my smile as long
as he could

He tried to make it easy
for me . . . But
it wasn't

Feeling outruns
me every time
. . . We come up
from our knees
composing light
People like us
can't go back . . . Except
in fairy tales and then
Only once

PROPHET AND LOSS

You can have
everything! . . . So
what the hell is this
about the chance
that it might
not last
forever?

. . . Are you mad?
How does the possibility
of being 'right' compare
to the loneliness of
being 'sorry'?

You think a girl who
makes you feel
 wonderful' comes
down the pike
every day, huh?
. . . You think because (you think)
she might leave you
in ten years
that it's not
worth a perfect
summer
together? . . . Are
you crazy?

You can have
everything . . . What the
hell are a few barren
New Year's Eves
compared to waking up
on Christmas morning
just once
with a girl who
makes you feel
wonderful?

Are you nuts? . . . Do
you really think
that letting her go
will ever stop
her from
leaving
you?

THE GOODTIME GIRLS

We're getting
older . . . You know that?
It doesn't matter how
good a liar
the skin is . . . I hardly
ever kiss frogs
any more

We are still
explorers . . . the journey (now)
continues down and
back . . . *Who could have told us*
then that we'd
be left with daughters
we couldn't
understand?

We're getting
better . . . You know that?
It doesn't matter
that the cops get
younger
every day . . . We have lost
our taste for
civil disobedience . . . But

We are still
fighting a
revolution . . . The issue (now)
continues in and
blazes . . . *Who could have told us*
then that we'd be
left with lovers
we couldn't
love?

WEREN'T WE SOMETHING?

Weren't we something?
. . . There were millions of us
A pack of hometown
skin . . . A gang of
middle income
outlaws . . . As classic
as the crew
neck

We fought against the war
(the Asian one)
It was (after all) a hometown massacre
We set out to show
the system
that it didn't
work . . . (we
were proof of
that)

We were really
something . . . You mighta
heard about us on the
news, huh? . . . They caught us trying
to put out the war with love . . . Too
young to touch each other but old enough
to die . . . That's what they said
A lot of us did both . . . Too soon . . . Too much

We smoked a lot of grass
It wasn't very strong
and neither were
we . . . But we set out
to show the world
that something
was wrong . . . (we were
proof of
that)

There were millions of us
Long hair was our signature
(no handwriting is the same)
We grew up in the sixties
We wore flowers in our hair
(you've seen the photographs)

We were just like you
. . . Only
different

Geordie Hormel

ANDREW

Andrew goes home
to his magazine
worshiping pressed pulp
filled with airbrushed images of naked women
putting girls before gods
(That human mistake)

. . . It's hard to love one woman
When you want all women

CAROLYN

Go ahead, Carolyn
Gather up the extra change
Save the extra nickels now
so that they may add
up to quarters later when
quarters will only be
worth a
nickel

Your fear of being poor
later is
making you
poor now

Buy the blue bathing suit
will you? . . . What treasure
will it be
later when you
want it
now?

You rob your youth
with the fear of not being
young . . . You just exchange
one poverty for
another . . . Your fear of
growing old is making
you
old

No amount of money
later is worth
that blue bathing suit
now

Some Robin Hood you are to
steal from the young Carolyn
treasures that will be useless to
the older
Carolyn

No matter what they promised
you . . . If you save it all to have it
then . . . You won't
have it
now

SIXTEEN YEARS AGO

Sixteen years ago
I was
Sixteen years old
. . . God was still a young man then
It was half past
July

My womb was still
uncharted
. . . Waiting for some
Magellan . . . My
body had just begun
its business
with my
heart

"Will you lay down
with me?" . . . That's what
he said . . . "Will you
be the girl
in my old
photographs?"

He opened his mouth
on the land
above my heart
. . . His right hand
Reached in
And touched me
right on the
memory

MOLLY MET A BOY TODAY

Molly met a boy today
that she has
loved all her life'
I know that isn't
possible . . . But
it's true

She can't draw a map
for you or
take you back
through their native
hands . . . But

She learned something
today . . . That I
could never
teach her . . . She
learned that she can
love someone 'all her
life' in an hour . . . And
that life provides us
with a memory
of places where we've
never been and
may never
go again

Some people
earn a place in our
past without
being there . . . Things
like that don't
really happen . . . But
they happen
all the
time

NIGHTSCHOOL

Ah, could we bring down the house
We let the night design itself
We let fate perform
unrehearsed
We let devotion
find its own
gods . . . We are mastered
by a leader who will not yield
to the
human form

It isn't a mistake
that music has muscle
. . . The velocity of thighs
is primal
. . . We were passing
for black . . . All
our prayers were
historic . . . Life is
a theater
of
chance . . . It did not
surprise us that the
evening was ours . . . Only
that the morning
cleared its throat
like a teacher . . .
We had to
earn our daily

bread . . . It isn't a
mistake that the sun
comes up every
day . . . That the morning
light catches up
upon (even) the veteran
magician and plays
upon his different
drum

Ah, could we bring down the
house? . . . we will let
the night eclipse the
authority of light
until the darkness shames the sun again
. . . We will let
our ends foster
their own means and
never will we
promise you a
Heaven that can be
mastered
by governments
who yield to
the human
form . . . It isn't a mistake
that we 'wake up' in
the morning

THE BODY

I celebrate
the body . . . It has
teeth . . . Its desire
is to be
hungry . . . Its
hunger is
to be
food

Passion
isn't a
particular
skill . . . It
is just a
night blindness . . . It
has a
murderer's
nerve . . . The
body has an
instinct for
crime . . . It has
a treasure
of lonely
talent

I celebrate
the body . . . it has
a fist . . . Its
business is to

make life and
love . . . The cell
has no discrimination
. . . It fights
death to
the
last
grave

Feeling
isn't a particular
skill . . . It is just
a voice that
asks for
attention . . . The
body has
a Mother
too . . . The heart
is a parent
. . . Selfish and
tired like anyone
who works
too
much . . . The brain
is just another
form of
government . . . But
the heart has

a red
gun . . . It reigns
like royalty
without a
bullet

I celebrate the body
. . . It has
hands
Its dream is
to be desired . . . Its
desire is to
be dreamed

Death is not
a particular
skill . . . It is
just a slight
exchange
of
power . . . The body
has no final
enemy . . . It
joins at
another root and
comes up
smiling and
hungry

WHAT IT FEELS LIKE NOW

There are so many things going on
But nothing is happening
. . . I'm high
But I'm not flying
I'm tough but
I'm not
strong

I feel a lot
but it isn't
good . . . So

Be careful
I can give you everything
you ever wanted
But
you can't keep it
or ever
use it
again

GOING PUBLIC

I suppose it would be easier to love a hundred men
I could divide my loyalty
Give less to more
. . . I could Xerox Valentines
And even with the paper work
the extra gas
the mileage on my smile . . . Still
it might be an advantage to love a lot of men a little
To give each one just enough of a voice
so that I might hear them if they called
and wouldn't miss them if they didn't
Sure . . . I wouldn't climb the sky as often
Neither would I fear the falling
Neither would I slap so cruelly on the ground
Yeah . . . Even with the added responsibility
of remembering all those names and birthdays
Even with the risk of utter mediocrity
Even with the wear and tear on all my vital parts
. . . I think it may be easier
to love a lot of men a little
than to love just one man
a lot

TWO WEEKS TOMORROW

It will be two weeks tomorrow
I made it through
two Saturday nights
so far . . . almost

It hurts like hell
But I'm going to get away
this time

I go out every night now
I have to for awhile
. . . I can still smell him
on the pillowcase . . . Even
now the heat rises from
his side of the
covers . . . He hasn't really
left yet and the
scraps make me
cry . . . The bed feels like a vacant crib

I'll make it this time
. . . I've been careful to stay away
from radios . . . One
song leads to
another . . . The words can ambush you
and pretty soon
if you don't watch out
you're back on music again . . . especially

the old songs . . . One small arrow
and you're on the ground
. . . You have to stay awake
when you're
running

I'm easy to reach these days
I don't put up much of a fight
One hug and you can have me
It doesn't even hurt (too much) and
I won't even tell you why
because I can't . . . And
I won't ever leave you
I won't go home again
(. . . at least not tonight) Because
in the morning it will be two weeks
since I said I never wanted to see him again
and this time he
believed me

THE LAST PAGE

Here we are at the 'end'
. . . But
It isn't over